INTRODUCTION

Every business knows the importance of social media for their marketing campaigns. Social media provides the opportunity to create a potentially viral message, to build powerful relationships with fans and leads, and to get feedback from that audience.

But social media is only one tool that the digital age provides us with when it comes to reaching large audiences and building deeper relationships with them. The smart marketers know that the key to great success online is to use all of these tools together. To see them like pieces in a jigsaw puzzle that are endlessly more effective when used in a combined manner.

The missing piece of the puzzle for many creators? Social messaging apps.

Social messaging apps are of course such things as WhatsApp, Facebook Messenger, Skype, Instagram, and iMessage. Even good old-fashioned SMS should be counted in there!

This is an option that has been available to marketers for decades now. And yet it is one that is very commonly overlooked by businesses. This is a huge missed opportunity however, seeing as social messaging might just be one of the most powerful options there *is* for marketers. This ebook wil explain why that is, and show you how to tap into the ful potential of this hugely beneficial strategy.

The Power of Social Messaging Apps

Chapter 1

Perhaps the question should not be "why use social messaging apps," but rather "why isn't everyone already doing it?" What is it about this form of marketing that has made it such a little-known secret among top marketers?

Perhaps it's because – as with so many things – creators are too determined to focus on quantity over quality. What does that mean?

Essentially, many creators wil consider a marketing strategy only if they think it can make a huge impact on their numbers. They want "ROI." They want their hard work to pay off. And so focus on the kind of work that is easily quantifiable.

Here, social messaging falls down a little. After all, you wil typically only send a WhatsApp to *one* person at a time. And that person is an already established lead: it is someone whose number you already have in your database, which means it's someone who already new about your business.

Therefore, WhatsApp involves engaging in a lot of effort in order to send a message to just one person, who was already on your list. Your numbers don't go up, and your marketing department has nothing to show for the work!

Compare that to a single Facebook post, which in theory can lead to thousands of new contacts in a matter of hours, and it becomes apparent that social messaging apps just don't have quite the same appeal for a lot of companies.

But that is entirely *missing the point*.

The point of social messaging apps is not to try and get a large quantity of new customers. Rather, it is about building the **quality** of your existing leads. And it's about conversions.

Developing Relationships

A lead is a customer, client, or *potential* customer/client that you have a relationship with. This is someone that you can contact, meaning that you own their contact details, and meaning that they are already familiar with your business. In most cases, they should already have given you *permission* to message them.

When we buy from a company, we wil typically go through a four stages which are commonly referred to by marketers as AIDA.

That means:

Awareness

Interest

Desire

Action

That's awareness of the product, interest in the product, desire for the product, and then the final purchase. If you think of traditional social media marketing techniques as being predominantly aimed at the first two points, social messaging marketing is about the latter two.

What's more, is that social messaging helps to increase familiarity, trust, and authority: three things that *help* to lubricate the process and encourage a lead to move from the first stage to the latter.

You'l col ect leads by making sales, by getting customers to sign up for various newsletters etc., and through the use of chatbots and comments. We wil discuss all of these topics later in the book.

But once you have the lead, you can't just expect that to lead to sales. And nor should you immediately dive in and try to sel something.

Think of this a little like dating. Imagine that you have noticed someone in a bar (awareness), gotten to talking (interest), and then given them your number. They are now a lead.

What do you do next? You message them!

Wait for them to message you, and you might wel have lost that prospective date entirely. Worse, is if you invite them over for sex. They hardly know you! So all they're going to do is get creeped out, delete your number, and potentially call the police if you bother them again. Not good. You can't ask for a big "transaction" like this without first establishing rapport, trust, and a mutual attraction.

You know what else doesn't work? Sending the new prospective date a series of automated emails designed to work for every type of person. It's not exactly personal, and they'l smel this a mile off.

They're not getting to *know you* any better.

Sales is the same. If you wait for a sale to just "happen" once you have your lead, then you wil likely lose that person. Likewise, you can't expect someone simply *knowing* about your business to be enough to then try and sel to them. Even showing moderate interest is not enough.

They have to not only desire the product or service, but also feel safe in the knowledge that if they pay you, you wil deliver. They need to believe that the product or service wil be just as you describe it.

And they need to know you're not going to then sel your contact details.

How do you get someone to "know you" in both scenarios? You message them! And you have an *actual conversation*. This is huge.

There are other reasons that you might be worried about using Messenger or WhatsApp in business.

Perhaps you're concerned about privacy, or perhaps you don't know how to go about it. Wel don't worry, all of that is going to be explained and fixed over the coming chapters. You'l learn how to get people to give you their contact details **willingly** and then contact **you** in order to ask just the right questions that wil allow you to sel to them!

More Benefits

Convenience and Immediacy

On top of this, text or instant messaging marketing is a form of marketing that occurs right in our pockets. This means you'l be reaching people when they're out and about, or when they're browsing the web during the day. This has a much more sensitive temporal aspect, and that means that if you message people during Saturday afternoon there's a chance they'l look at it while they're out shopping which isn't generally the case even with e-mail which we normally assume can wait. That means you may even influence their buying behavior there and then – no need for them to remember anything in the first place.

Marketing to Short People

These days nearly everyone is texting from nippers to seniors - which makes text marketing a viable option no matter what your business is. However, it's also worth noting that some demographics use mobile phones even more than others and generally these are quite desirable demographics –

specifically teenagers with a healthy disposable income. This then means that you're reaching out to an audience that have few financial commitments but are starting to get money in their wallets. Better yet, most teens these days are using smartphones like iPhones which means that even if they aren't out shopping they'l be able to head online and visit your site there and then - especially as smartphones handily turn URLs into hyperlinks that open in the native browser. Combine this with multimedia benefits of smart messaging and you have a whole world of marketing possibilities.

Facebook Reach is Shrinking

There's another reason that more and more people are turning to Messenger and other forms of instant messaging: Facebook's organic reach has *massively* shrunk. There was a time that you could post something to your Facebook group, and you would then find that a large number of people who fol owed you would see it.

Today, that's not quite so true. Users started getting fed up with only seeing posts from businesses and never seeing anything from their friends, and as such Facebook adapted and started showing fewer

business posts. The fact that this also drove more companies to use their expensive advertising platform was a nice added bonus!

Thus companies are looking for other ways to reach Facebook's community. And one of the most powerful ways to do that is through instant messaging.

Facebook Messenger and WhatsApp – The Big Ones

Chapter 2

Now you know a bit about why you should be getting involved in social messaging for your business, the next question is what apps and tools you should be using to do that. In this chapter, we'l look at the top options.

Facebook Messenger

This is the big one. Facebook Messenger is used by 1.3 bil ion people, which is a large percentage of people on the planet. Despite this, only 31% of businesses are currently using Facebook Messenger for marketing purposes. That should tel you that this is a huge untapped potential, and that right now you can very easily stand out among the crowd.

Facebook Messenger is so powerful thanks to its many different features and tools, not to mention its amazing integration with Facebook itself.

Here are just some of the things you can do with Facebook Messenger: **Get Contacted Directly From Your Page:** With Facebook Messenger, anyone who views your page wil be able to easily get in touch and message you. This is a fantastic, ready-made sales funnel. You can create and share a post from your page, or even post an ad. This wil generate more traffic to your page, where you can promote your product, and then all the customer has to do is to click the button to send you an IM!

Facebook Ads: Facebook Messenger now also integrates beautiful y with Facebook Ads. Specifically, you can set Facebook Messenger as a "Call to Action," meaning that as soon as someone clicks your ad, they wil be taken to Messenger where they can get in touch. This is powerful stuff.

Call Contacts: If you're speaking to someone through Facebook Messenger and you think there's a high chance of making a sale, then Messenger wil allow you to very easily contact that person to make a sale or strengthen your relationship with that lead.

Employ Bots: We'l look at this more in a future chapter, but by using bots you can answer questions that your visitors have automatically and thereby provide the kind of one-to-one service that you perhaps don't have the resources to provide otherwise. This can help to direct your visitors down a sales-funnel and it can also help make your business look far more attentive in the way it handles queries and visitors.

Add to Your Website: You can easily add a Facebook chat box to your website, which wil make it easy for you to col ect new contacts, and at the same time to add new people to your list.

Plugins: Facebook has some more very powerful plugins that wil easily integrate with a WordPress website. One of the best is the Checkbox Plugin. This allows you to col ect contacts to receive messages from you or a bot in Messenger and to get their permission.

This means you can col ect contact information in JUST the same way that you would be col ecting it for an email mailing list. In fact, you can combine both those things at once.

Another great plugin is the Send to Messenger plugin. This one triggers an authentication event in your webhook, allowing you to pass data to know the user that clicked the link.

The MessageUsplugin works as you might expect too, allowing users to start up a conversation with you or your bot from anywhere on your site by clicking a button.

***

Facebook is predominantly intended as a platform for social interactions with existing, real-world contacts. That means friends and family. Users often don't take that kindly to being messaged by businesses, and likewise Facebook itself wil clamp down on companies that abuse the service.

But although all of that is true, it's also very true that sending lots of messages in this way has become somewhat more commonplace. People expect it on Facebook to an extent, and in many cases the client or customer wil actually *initiate* the conversation with the business. For those reasons, you might find that Facebook offers a slightly more receptive audience than some other platforms.

Combined with the significant

WhatsApp

WhatsApp has a lot of strong things going for it when it comes to social message marketing, but also a few drawbacks that can leave some businesses understandably apprehensive.

The big benefit of course is that WhatsApp is about as raw and immediate as any form of marketing could be. WhatsApp is a platform that we predominantly use in order to talk with friends and family.

These days, most of us wil use it *instead* of SMS!

Thus, when we get a message on WhatsApp, we wil almost *always* check it immediately. From there, a message from a business is going to stand out to a large extent.

WhatsApp also has a number of useful features just like Facebook. You can embed links and media in messages, and you can call people using WiFi.

The other great thing about WhatsApp is that all you need to start messaging someone on it is their number. If you have their mobile number, you'l be able to add them on the platform and get in touch.

Whereas Facebook Messenger requires the use of ready-made plugins then, you'l be able add someone on WhatsApp without explicitly gaining permission or using any third party tools (though you should like not do the former except for in extreme cases).

The best way to col ect contacts for WhatsApp is to simply ask your customers or your leads to fil in their mobile number when they fil out any other form. You can then include a checkbox stating that it's okay – or otherwise – for you to message them that way.

Of course you stil need to be very careful here. A lead must be highly engaged to be happy with a WhatsApp message – especially as they may wel forgot that they ticked the box!

The other option is to let customers contact you through WhatsApp for various purposes. This works in just the same way as providing a phone number for a customer or client to call if they have questions, except you wil handle the conversation through WhatsApp. Many people find this is very reassuring as they might be anxious of speaking in person, whereas WhatsApp lets them get answers without having to speak up or get out of their comfort zone.

As we go through this book, we'l see more potential uses of every type of social messaging platform –

including WhatsApp.

While social messaging marketing wil largely refer to Facebook and WhatsApp, it can actually encompass a number of other platforms and strategies…

SMS

SMS marketing means sending messages to your potential buyers in order to tel them about your offers and deals. SMS marketing is popular with companies because texts have such a high open-rate.

However, market research conclusively shows that people are aggravated by text messages from businesses and there are some stringent laws in the US that prevent you from abusing this technique.

This form of marketing has many of the same benefits and weaknesses as does WhatsApp marketing.

A few key things can ensure that your SMS marketing is wel received and not frustrating: Get permission from your recipients – Get people to sign up for your SMS alerts rather than surprising them. This is the *only* way to avoid this strategy damaging your brand's reputation.

Be respectful – Think careful y about how often you're going to message and at what times. People won't appreciate getting three texts a day from you and they certainly don't want to hear about pizza at 5am on Sunday morning.

Know your audience – The key is to send the right message, to the right person, at the right time.

Make sure that your message is on-point and that you have enough information about the recipients to assume that they may be interested in your offer. If you have a really good system going, you can even message your customers to say happy birthday and offer a discount!

Provide value – The main kind of message that your users are wil ing to receive is a discount or special offer. This way you are providing actual value by saving them money and you can link them straight to your app where they can redeem the offer.

Be creative – While it's not always appropriate, you can use SMS in creative ways to increase engagement. Potential options include running competitions, sending rhymes or using ASCII art. If you can make your recipient smile, this wil go a long way to improving the reception of your message.

You have to be extremely careful with SMS marketing then, but by thinking logically and understanding its limitations, you can stil be successful. No one wil begrudge being wished happy birthday by a company.

Likewise, if the lead has actually *interacted with you personally* in any meaningful way, then SMS and WhatsApp by extension become more viable. For instance, you can message a customer who is in your store, and you'l then be able to strike up a conversation. You can likewise message a customer to confirm they have ordered a product and include the note to "respond to this message with any questions." Again, this can use a non-aggravating message in order to begin a longer communication thread with more potential sales and marketing opportunities.

NFC and Proximity Marketing

Something else similar but more obscure is "NFC marketing." NFC stands for "Near Field Communication" and this is the ability of your phone to transfer data simply by being in close proximity to another device. NFC marketing could potentially allow people to open your website or app by just *tapping* their mobile device against a poster in your store, or to check themselves in on Facebook. Al you need is an RFID chip and these are very small and cost effective. This is an early technology though and not something that people are getting involved in in a big way just yet. The potential for col ecting data is somewhat huge though!

NFC can also be used as a form of proximity marketing, meaning that you can send messages to users as they walk past certain points in your store. Other examples of proximity marketing include marketing via Bluetooth or GSM. These methods have a lot of hurdles to overcome though, as people need to accept incoming Bluetooth requests for instance and it's really a little invasive. For now, you can generally ignore this type of marketing unless you have an extremely specific and creative use in mind.

Hopeful y if nothing else, this book has demonstrated to you already that you can get over many of the hurdles of social messaging marketing by thinking creatively.

Others

This is only just scratching the surface though! Here are some other platforms you can use social messaging through in order to reach out to your potential customers and clients: **Instagram:** Instagram has a direct messaging functionality that works similarly to Facebook's. This is actually no coincidence seeing as Facebook owns Instagram, and thus it should also come as no surprise to learn that Instagram and Facebook Messenger are closely integrated – you can answer Instagram messages right through Facebook!

Instagram's visual nature and excel ent ROI make it a popular choice among businesses, especially those with a very visual product or emotive message. The limitation has always been that you can't

place a link to buy a product in your image description. An easy solution though? Just place a note saying "DM for more." Then answer them on Facebook Messenger!

There are other powerful tricks you can use on Instagram too. One is to run a pol and this way see which of your fol owers answered. The reason this works so wel , is that you can then message – for example – only the fol owers that answered that they "would be interested in X product" and that way you're directly talking to a qualified lead!

Likewise, you can also invite users to ask you questions via the Sticker provided in Stories. Again, this gives you the opportunity to speak to those users directly as a fol ow up.

Skype: Skype is another very useful tool for business. You can easily message a lot of businesses that use Outlook or other Microsoft accounts, and this is a format where a lot of companies feel happy doing business. Send a WhatsApp message to the head of an accounting firm and they might wel be extremely annoyed, but if they receive a ping on Skype, this is a far more suitable environment and one that they can answer at their own leisure. Another strategy is to send an email and simply ask

"would it be okay if I messaged on Skype to continue this conversation?"

LinkedIn: LinkedIn's InMail has a number of highly powerful features that make it ideal for a number of marketing and business activities. One is InMail's ability to let you message 2nd and 3rd degree contacts. That means that as long as someone is connected to someone that *you* are connected to (a mutual connection), you can reach out to them. This in turn means you can message BIG influencers in your niche, potentially far huger than you might otherwise stand a chance of reaching. Add as many people as possible from your personal network and your list, and you wil that way be able to grow your network on LinkedIn and your reach to a massive extent.

The excel ent plugin called Rapportive (find it here: https://www.crunchbase.com/organization/rapportive) is also very useful. This tool wil allow you to see the LinkedIn details of anyone who messages you via Gmail, which means you can turn every new message into a new connection to then speak with.

Like Skype, LinkedIn is a platform that businesses use *in order* to network and find opportunities. So if you have a B2B service, then this is a great option for sending DMs.

***

This is really just scratching the surface of the social messaging apps out there. There are many more and essentially most social media platforms now have some form of social messaging. To that end, you should look at the platforms where your brand is thriving most and then explore the potential benefit of using social messaging as wel .

-

What is Conversational Commerce?

Chapter 4

Conversational commerce is a term that was initially coined by Uber's Chris Messina. You might know Uber as the taxi company that has absolutely *exploded* in the last decade, to the point that it has completely disrupted its industry and even gotten some analysts and economists pretty worried! So this guy knows what he's talking about, and social messaging apps are CLEARLY a big part of his strategy.

So what does all this mean? How can you employ it into your own strategies?

Essentially, conversational commerce describes the rapidly rising trend of interacting between businesses and clients/customers through social apps and tools. That includes custom apps, SMS, and even telepresence like Skype and Zoom. Via these methods, consumers get to discuss matters with company representatives. To get customer support, to ask pertinent questions about their products and services, and even make purchases.

This completely changes the game in a profound way that may help to take your business to a completely different level. Why? Because you can now speak *directly* with a customer, one-to-one.

While this might seem like a lot of effort, it does several things for your relationship: It reassures your customers and clients that your business is run by real people, and that they wil be able to get hold of you. This is huge, because it means that if someone were to have a problem with a product or service, they would be able to get in touch and get a useful response and hopeful y have the issue solved. That in turn creates a huge amount of additional trust in your business, meaning that they are FAR more likely to click "buy" and take a risk with their hard-earned cash.

It creates a sense of gratitude and obligation. Most of us are fairly humble. While there are certainly some entitled individuals out there (and we wil discuss how to deal with these types in future chapters), most people actually don't *expect* to get an answer from a big organization or company. We tend to think of professional organizations as being somehow "more important" than us, and as such, we are shy about asking for advice.

When a company actually takes the time to respond to a question, or even to send a marketing message in some cases, this can show that they care about the individual. Humbled, they might then feel someone "obligated" to buy – or at least feel far more inclined too, viewing your business as having "earned" them.

You'l can deal with issues and "barriers to sale" head on. A barrier to sale is anything that prevents a customer from wanting to do business with you. So for example, if someone were unsure which product out of a selection was right for them, then they might choose not to buy. But by using chat, you can then answer the question for them, point them in the right direction, and hopeful y fil them with lots of confidence that wil help them to make a purchase.

You can even get the process started! That is to say that you can help someone begin fil ing out a form, or even talk them through the checkout process. "The answer to that question is X. Product Y

should be able to help you with that. Would you like me to add it to your cart?" This can drastically increase your conversion rate while *also* serving the client and giving them a good experience.

You can get feedback and very useful information. A very strong example might be to ask "I see you were looking at product X but didn't buy, what could I do to change your mind?" This can go as far as to convert an otherwise lost customer into a buyer. If not, it can give you valuable information that you can use to improve your products in future, and increase your chances of making more sales next time.

Generating Good Wil

Another fantastic benefit of using conversational commerce, is that it allows you to generate goodwil .

One of the secrets to success in business is to "overdeliver." That's to do more than you promise, and more than you "have to," and thereby to pleasantly surprise the customer. People love being surprised in this manner.

To do this, you can try messaging someone to wish them happy birthday, to thank them for buying from you, or to check if they have access to everything they need/thank them for signing up to the site. Make this a personal message and they wil likely be extremely touched that you took the time out.

I STILL remember as a child once signing up to a newsletter for a game I liked (*Abe's Odyssey*) and then getting a card from the company on my birthday. This was huge for me as a young fan!

While this might be impossible for some businesses to replicate owing to financial and time constraints, it's certainly NOT impossible to consider sending a Facebook message. And people wil really appreciate that and remember your business as a result.

How to Reach Out

Of course the problem with conversational commerce is starting that conversation in a way that doesn't upset or insult the user. Drop-off rates are huge when companies start sending unsolicited messages, and this is something that companies should think hard about.

The good news is that there are plenty of ways to safely start this kind of conversation.

One is to wait for the individual to contact you through your Facebook page or your website. A chat bot on your website can also help you do this. Another is to get them to sign up and "opt in" to your messages using the buttons we described before. You can also wait for them to contact you, and then message them back.

Another great strategy is to respond to a message that someone leaves on your wall but privately.

Al these things work and we'l discuss them more in future chapters. For now though, just know that there *are* plenty of good ways you can reach out to your clients and customers to begin this kind of conversational commerce – meaning you can take advantage of all those huge benefits we've touched on so far.

OR you could start sel ing directly...

Messaging Apps for Sales

Chapter 5

So social messaging for marketing is all about creating deeper relationships with your existing customers and clients. This lets you transform those leads into qualified leads.

But how do you then turn qualified leads into buyers? The great news is that this is the perfect fit for social messaging apps as wel !

How to Sel Through Social Messaging Apps

As we have somewhat touched upon already, social messaging apps are ideal for sel ing because they allow you to answer the questions of the client, and to convince them to think about making a purchase.

When we discussed the different platforms for social messaging, we saw some of the ways that we could strike up conversations with people using those platforms. For instance, you can message someone about a post they left on your Facebook wall, or you can send an invoice or confirmation of some kind that includes the

The key is to not try and sel from this position right away. If you send the message "I see you posted on our wall, can I interest you in X product?" then you may wel get blocked.

However, if you send a message that asks a question and begins a conversation, then you can use this to then *direct* that conversation toward a sale. Ask them why they feel that way, ask them what brought them to your site, and look for an opportunity to bring the conversation to products and services that you can provide. You can then begin with a gentle nudge, such as "have you considered X product?" or "did you know we sold Y?"

Another tip is to keep these messages short. Longer messages are off-putting for customers on these platforms, and especially if they aren't expecting them. 2-3 sentences should be considered your maximum.

Upselling

Another great option for using social messaging is to "upsel ." That means that when someone buys something from your site, you then fol ow up immediately with the offer to sel something else. This can be done via a chat window, so that when someone buys your ebook, you then mention that they have qualified for a discount on your supplement range as wel if they would be interested?

This direct conversation (even if it is handled by a bot) makes it extremely easy for someone to buy from you.

Instant Engagement

It's common knowledge that when someone lands on your website, you wil normally have about 10

seconds to convince them to stay. If they can't see what they're looking for immediately, then chances are that they wil leave.

So how do you prevent this? One option is to have a chat window appear *immediately* and ask if it can help the visitor. This gives them an immediate answer to any questions they might have, and prevents them from leaving out of confusion – one of the most paralyzing emotions that can completely destroy your sales otherwise!

Chatbots

Chapter 6

Imagine this scenario for a moment. It shouldn't be too far-fetched, seeing as it is the precise scenario a client of mine found themselves in.

This client had a successful fitness blog and YouTube channel. They'd done a fantastic job of building their audience and also increasing engagement to the point that people really wanted to connect and interact with them.

As such, their Facebook page grew pretty much all on its own. This led to them getting LOTS of messages on Facebook from people who wanted to complement them on their work, ask questions, and even ask if they were available for personal training!

But this person had multiple business interests. They were also running several other online businesses, and they spent a lot of time coaching clients, writing training programs, and running the blog and YouTube. Those question went unanswered.

This had two big impacts:

It hurt the content creator's reputation by making them appear to not care about their audience. They would quickly gain a reputation among their folowers as someone that didn't answer fans, and that therefore was not worth messaging. Engagement was dropping.

It meant they would miss out on a huge number of potential clients, which could have been enough to allow them to drastically increase their rates. After all, these clients were so keen on the idea of getting training from them that they sought them out through Facebook and messaged them personally! This is an *extremely* qualified lead, and someone who would likely be happy to pay a lot for a good service.

The solution that I provided was to get a chatbot. The chatbot would then man the Messenger and be able to answer simple questions. What's more, is that it could politely explain to users that the person

was inundated with messages and unfortunately had a hard time answering everyone directly.

However, if they wanted a consultation, they could do so by signing up at X address.

This created a simple sales funnel using entirely existent materials, that quickly helped the client of mine to develop a massively successful business model. They gained lots of new leads, which allowed them to drastically *increase* the amount they charged for training sessions.

In turn, they were then able to spend less time writing programs, and more time working on the content of the site – which in turn helped them to increase their exposure even more. Today that client is an Instagram influencers that gets paid thousands of dol ars to wear sports gear during workouts. It worked out okay for them!

Sel ing Directly

Here's something else you may not have realized you could do with a social messaging campaign: process orders *entirely* through your app!

Several companies are now doing this, even using Chatbots to completely automate the process. In particular, this option is popular among restaurants and fast food joints. Taxi firms are also embracing the concept.

Here, the customer wil usually already have an account with the business that has their delivery address and payment detail stored. They wil then send a message through Facebook Messenger,

WhatsApp, or a bespoke app (see the next chapter) stating that they would like to order food. This wil then begin a scripted sequence where the bot wil ask which items, what sizes/toppings/extras, when they'd like it, and how they'd like to pay. They wil then ask the user to confirm, and within a minute, the transaction wil be over.

This is a very natural, easy, and FAST way for people to buy from you, and that makes them instantly more inclined to take that strategy. It's also a very modern approach that can help to improve your reputation, and

Companies such as ClickSend (www.clicksend.com) make this very quick and simple to set up.

If you want to start increasing your brand visibility, gaining more sales and generally taking your business to the next level then you *absolutely need an app*.

There was a point about 20 years ago, when every business started recognizing how badly they needed a website. There was a sudden 'rush' that fol owed as every business quickly started building websites and hiring designers. Today there's absolutely no question that every business needs a website and that without one, they can't expect to reach nearly as many people or secure half as many sales.

Everyone has been a little slower on the uptake this time around but now we find ourselves in the exact same position with apps. In other words, if you run a business then you *need* an app just as badly as you need a website. And as with websites, that need is only going to grow and grow as technology progresses.

At this point, you might be wondering what use an app might have for you. Wel , try asking a company like Starbucks or Amazon and they'l tel you how they make *far* more sales directly as a result of their app. Or maybe you could turn to blogs like IGN and they'd tel you how their apps help them to connect with their audience and promote their posts.

But of course an app can ALSO be another option for promoting your business through social messaging. That's because a lot of companies create apps that have messaging functionality *built into them* which actually has a huge number of benefits even *over* the regular features.

What An App Can Do For You

So a good place to start then is by asking what an app can do for you.

For starters, an app can of course improve your visibility and help impress your visitors. Having an app makes your company seem more modern and more capable *and* it means that people can now discover you via the Google PlayStore and/or iTunes store.

On top of this though, having an app also gives you a new way to communicate directly with your customers. This is thanks to something called the "push notification." Push notifications essentially allow your apps to post updates that appear right at the top of the phone and on the lock screen and your app doesn't even have to be open to do this. That means you can tel your fans about your special offers or your latest blog post and they won't even have to be using the phone to see it! Unlike email marketing, you don't have to compete with thousands of other marketers and you don't need to worry about the spam filter. For these reasons in fact, push notifications have an open rate of 92%! No email campaign wil ever come close to that.

Of course, when you use other social messaging apps, those apps wil also *include* a push notification when a new message is received. However, you'l find that this isn't as impactful seeing as those notifications are competing with notifications from *other* users. This is compared with a notification that you control in its entirety on a channel that you *own*.

Then you have things like GPS. You can actually use this to direct your users directly to your store if you have a brick and mortar business! Or you can use it to send context sensitive push notifications –

i.e. when someone is outside your restaurant you can offer them to come in for a drink. You can also use this information during a discussion (though be careful not to be creepy in this way!) Apps also let you make direct sales in a very convenient manner. Using in-app purchases or PayPal, you can let your users look through your products and place orders at their leisure. Likewise, they can order food or book a table and they won't even have to leave the app.

Starbucks uses this in a very smart way by letting users say what time they want their coffee and then pay through the app. That way, instead of having to queue on their commute to work, they can just pop in to col ect the coffee with their name on it!

Imagine being able to promote something via a push notification, then letting that notification take your user *directly* to your beautiful y designed app where they can buy your product with one click and without having to enter any of their details! Or letting them click to start up a conversation with you. This works for physical products but it also works like a charm for digital products and is the perfect way for you to monetize your website and sel more ebooks!

Even if it weren't for all these powerful benefits, an app simply provides a more tailor-made experience for your users to read content on their phones. They won't be distracted by other websites and everything wil load much more quickly.

And here's another thing you may not have considered: that you can actually use an app you built in order to send someone Facebook Messenger or WhatsApp and to begin a conversation with you! This is a great way to integrate social messaging with an app you created for marketing.

Now what you're probably thinking is that this is all great… but beyond your capabilities. How can you build an app on your own with no experience?

Actually, that bit is easy! And I'm going to show you why…

Using App Builders to Create Professional Apps in 3 Minutes or Less What if I told you you could create a professional looking mobile app in under 3 minutes?

The good news? It's completely true!

The trick is simply to use an app builder, which is a piece of software written specifically to make it easier for you to build apps in just a few minutes and then package them ready for iOS *and* Android.

You can of course go the traditional route to create your mobile app which wil mean coding it yourself in Java, Objective-C or Swift. This means learning a whole language for most people though as wel as familiarizing themselves with the Android or iOS SDK. Then they have to set up their IDE (wil you use Android Studio or Eclipse?) and install the latest virtual devices for testing. You'l need to learn how a manifest file works and how to set up your private key sign… and that's all assuming your computer is able to run all that stuff (it needs a lot of space if nothing else and you can only develop for iOS this way on a Mac).

So… probably not, right?

Using an app builder isn't as flexible or powerful but the good news is that many of them are designed specifically for internet marketing purposes. That means that the functionality they *do* provide is exactly what you're likely to need to promote your website, digital products or business.

Here are just some of the best tools that wil get you started…

Appatap

http://Appatap.com/appatapoto.html

To use Appatap, you begin by selecting the app template you want. As you can imagine, this is essentially the layout you want and wil define the broad purpose of your app as wel as where all the individual elements are going to go.

Next you change the images you want and the text you want and you select the features you're going to need. The features available include:

Shopping cart

Maps and GPS

In-app purchases

PayPal

Push notifications

Chat

Image galleries

RSS feeds

You pick and choose these as you need them – so if you want to create an app to promote your blog you'l probably just go with the RSS feed to show your content and then use a push notification to alert your users about new content.

On the other hand, if you want to let people order your products you'l want to use the shopping cart, the in-app purchases and the PayPal support.

Once all that is done, you simply press publish and your app wil be packaged ready for the Play Store or iTunes! The other great thing about this, is that you can actually use **AppInstitute**

https://appinstitute.com/

This is another powerful app maker for iOS and Android that lets you get started quickly and provides a number of enterprise-centric features. That includes a very powerful booking feature, a loyalty feature, push notifications, and the ability to chat with a member of your team. Al the stuff we need in other words! It's not free (though you can build a trial app for free) but is relatively inexpensive at $42 per month.

AppyPie

https://www.appypie.com/

AppyPie is a similar app builder that focusses primarily on simplicity. It's great for making specific

"types" of app, but you can use this to create a general business app if you so wish, **Shoutem**

http://www.shoutem.com/

We could keep going forever, so we'l put just one more item on this list: Shoutem. This is a very crisp and nicely made platform that you can use to make similarly attractive and modern apps for your business. It lets you stay in touch with your users using all the same features as others on this list, but also has powerful Shopify integration for sel ing from an eCommerce store directly!

***

The other huge difference between creating an app for marketing purposes and using a more traditional form of social messaging marketing, is that creating an app comes with an implicit permission to contact your potential buyers.

In other words, if you message someone on WhatsApp without their explicit permission, then you might risk getting told off and upsetting the customer. However, if you message someone directly through your app – this is something that the user is likely expecting. By downloading the app, they

demonstrate that they are happy to receive more communication from you, which entirely changes the relationship while allowing you to benefit from *all* the same features.

We've only touched briefly on what apps can do for you though and how you can start making the most of them.

Right now, only the very biggest and smartest companies are taking ful advantage of mobile marketing with their own apps and mobile sites. If you want to get ahead of the competition, then this is a great way to do it and it wil lead to an instant increase in sales and engagement.

Collecting and Managing Contact Details

Chapter 8

One of the biggest challenges you'l face when it comes to your social messaging marketing, is col ecting the contact details of the people that you wil be sel ing to and getting their permission to send them marketing materials.

So how do you do this? There are a number of tools and strategies that lend themselves perfectly to using social messaging apps. Here are just a few.

Messenger Specific Facebook Ads

We touched on this notion already, but essentially it is possible to create Facebook Ads where the goal is to trigger a Facebook message. This is a bril iant way to get more people on your list so that you can start contacting them and encouraging conversions.

Messenger On Your Website

The same goes for adding Messenger to your website. By using Facebook's "Customer Chat Plugin,"

you'l be able to directly link Messenger to your website. That means your visitors wil be greeted by a pop-up as soon as they arrive, helping guide them to your checkout page.

What's great about this, is that the stream of the chat wil automatical y be moved over to Messenger on Facebook, so you can continue right where you left off and find out just *why* they never clicked buy in the end!

Use Opt-In

Another option we have already touched on is the opt-in plugin. This is a simple checkbox you'l use on your email landing page that lets them *also* subscribe to your Messenger.

You can likewise do the same thing with WhatsApp in a less direct manner, by letting them enter their mobile number and tick a box stating that they're happy to be contacted.

Rapportive

As mentioned, Rapportive is a powerful tool for growing your Instagram Inmail contacts in particular.

This one works by letting you see the details of anyone that messages you on LinkedIn – so you only have to click to quickly add them to your network!

Start Up a Chat

If someone comments on your post or photo, then you should respond. If this goes to two or more returns, then you can always just suggest that you *continue* the chat on social messaging. The same works for Instagram.

Better yet then, why not post on someone *else's*

Invitation

It might be that a lot of people would happily chat with you or DM you, but that the idea simply hadn't crossed their mind. Run a competition or just invite people to get in touch through a post, and you'l find your inbox swel s fast!

MobileMonkey

A number of tools including MobileMonkey (https://mobilemonkey.com/), ManyChat (https://manychat.com/), and WhatsHelp (https://whatshelp.io/) can help you to "generate leads on autopilot". These work by letting you convert anyone who comments on one of your posts to Messenger contacts.

Basically this works by using a bot which wil automatically message anyone who answers a set post or question. The message wil link back to your post, ensuring they know why they're being contacted and using that same "excuse" method we have used in person previously.

This is a bril iant way to grow your audience without even trying!

Customer Match

Customer Match is a tool that uses an API to send messages based on the first name, last name, or phone number. If it finds a match – a person who is on your list but isn't also on your Facebook Messenger, then it wil send a request for them to opt-in.

How successful you are when you message someone on a social messaging app wil come down partly to how you conduct yourself and your communication skil s. Keep in mind that you are messaging someone through a platform that is ostensibly meant for friends and family, and that they may take offense at this.

This is a delicate line to walk then, and you need to be careful about how you phrase your messages in order to get the best response.

Use Their Name and be Personal

A lot of bulk e-mail services and programs wil allow you to insert the name of the person you're emailing which of course wil help them to spot the message in their inbox. We have been conditioned to look for our name in blocks of text and so this is a good way to make your message stand out initially. Don't over-do this one though, it has been used a lot and so it's actually starting to be seen as a sign that a message is a piece of marketing. 'Hey, John!' is a subject line that John has seen to often, so use it subtly and creatively. (Using their title, or mentioning something about them like the website they own can be more effective for instance.)

The same goes for your social messaging – try to refer to the individual by name, to demonstrate that you are not just sending out large amounts of spam content without giving any thought to who is on the receiving end!

Another tip in this same vein, is to try and do your research where possible. If someone messages you on Facebook through your page, you can view their profile in order to that way get an idea of who they are and what their interests might be. A great option at this point then is to **Involve Them**

Using the recipient's name or details is one way to make them feel involved and make them assume that the message is actually relevant to them. There are other ways to involve them though too and all of these can be equally as powerful if not more so.

One method for instance is to ask for advice. If your message says something like "Could you please help me come up with some ideas?" then you'l find you get a surprising number of readers. People love being asked for help/advice (we're all narcissists deep down), but more to the point this is the kind of strategy that we're not used to seeing from businesses and that makes it pique our interest more.

Be Honest

Another strategy is to just be honest but to set yourself apart. People are pretty savvy and desensitised these days when it comes to things like e-mail marketing or social messaging, so rather than trying to get in under their radar, why not just say "I have something great to offer and I think you should take a look." It's refreshing, it's honest, and when they do click on the link to open it they're going to be much more open to whatever you're sel ing than they would be if they felt they had been tricked.

Likewise, when someone signs up to your Messenger, make sure they do so under no false pretenses.

You intend on sel ing to them? Then *say* that!

Cold Sales

Every now and then, you might decide you want to try messaging a potential lead "cold." That means that they have not given you any explicit or implicit permission to message, and you are not in any way continuing a "conversation" or answering something they sent.

When doing this, it is stil important to ensure that you have permission to contact the individual, and that they are genuinely engaged and interested in your brand.

It's also important to keep your message short, brief, and to the point. Start with a phrase like "As a loyal customer," or "Thank you for liking our page!" This can help to get the conversation off on the right foot, and can help to explain away the message out of the blue a little.

You should stil keep your messages extremely short, and should aim to ask *one* question in them. This way, you wil get them to engage. That question should be something interesting, and it should be something that they can answer quickly with a "yes or no" answer.

Interestingly, you may have more luck if you try to get them to answer "no" rather than "yes." This is because we are asked to say "yes" to marketing messages too often and have become desensitized.

Answering "no" feels different and makes us sit up and take notice.

For example then, asking: "can you spare a moment?"

Is less likely to be successful than asking: "are you busy right now?"

Internal Uses, Providing Services, and More!

Chapter 10

There are countless more powerful ways that you can use social messaging in your business. Let's touch on just a few.

Making the Call

While using social messaging apps is very powerful when you type, they can be even more powerful when used to discuss something face-to-face over a video call. This way, you can persuade with your gestures, your tone of voice, and your physical demonstrations. It's much harder to say no to someone's face, and it's much easier to feel you trust someone that you can actually *see*!

Networking and Finding Business Partners

One particularly good reason to make a call via Facebook or Skype where possible, is so that you can network. While a customer or client might be reluctant to let you call them before you do business, you'l likely find that a fel ow business owner or marketer is much more likely to see this as a normal activity and therefore to actually respond to your requests.

This makes it ideal for influencer marketing then, or for finding a partner that can help you take your business further. The best part is that a lot of influencers and marketers aren't used to being messaged on Facebook or Instagram, and so this is more likely to get opened than a message by email.

If you then start up a call, you'l find you can build a much longer-lasting and more impactful relationship.

Providing Your Service

Another option that you might not have considered, is using Messenger or WhatsApp in order to actually *provide* the service. This IS the product then, and so it's also the perfect place to market it.

An example of this might be to sel some kind of course or training program that consists of sequenced messages through Facebook. Or alternatively, maybe you provide free consultation, coaching, or fitness training via WhatsApp!

You can also enhance your current service by adding a chat functionality. For example, Amazon Kindles have built-in tech support letting anyone call a member of staff to ask for help. You could offer something similar.

Or if you provide coaching face-to-face, then you could *also* supply some "aftercare" in the form of WhatsApp messages for a set number of interactions.

Internal Uses

Keep in mind as wel that social messaging apps have a ton of usefulness for organizations *internally*.

These are great for staying in touch with members of the team, and for col aborating remotely. You can use tools like Slack for this, or even just stick with Facebook Messenger and WhatsApp!

Group Chat

You can even use social messaging apps in order to sel to larger groups by creating a group chat. Of course, this is one way to more quickly market to a bigger audience, though you'l find this strategy can turn people off and cause them to leave your chat and then unsubscribe!

One way to prevent this is to make the message group a kind of "VIP" and very selective group that your audience wil be excited to be a part of – especially if you offer freebies and advice.

You can likewise use group chat when trying to sel something to a larger group. Perhaps you might have several managers from a business in here for example, and that way you increase your chances of a positive outcome.

Customer Service

You can use social messaging to provide after care and support for a wide range of different products and services, thereby ensuring that your support lasts long after the transaction has gone through.

This can also help to boost your reviews and gain more repeat business!

As you can see then, there are countless uses for social messaging apps for marketing and for business in general. I hope that this book has helped to open your eyes to some of those and to think outside the box with the way you use this tool. I hope it has *also* demonstrated to you just HOW powerful this tool is, and why it absolutely deserves a place in your arsenal. Now you know how to build an audience, message them for the highest chances of success, and use apps and tools to get more out of the strategy.

But ultimately it comes down to good old-fashioned conversation. It's a lost art in the world of internet marketing, if you're among the first to bring it back, then you are almost guaranteed success!

www.ingramcontent.com/pod-product-compliance
Lightning Source LLC
LaVergne TN
LVHW042112231224
799806LV00008B/344